habitat explorer

Coral Reef Explorer

Greg Pyers

www.raintreepublishers.co.uk
Visit our website to find out more information about **Raintree** books.

To order:
 Phone 44 (0) 1865 888112
 Send a fax to 44 (0) 1865 314091
Visit the Raintree Bookshop at **www.raintreepublishers.co.uk** to browse our catalogue and order online.

Published in 2004 by Heinemann Library
a division of Harcourt Education Australia,
18–22 Salmon Street, Port Melbourne Victoria 3207 Australia
(a division of Reed International Books Australia Pty Ltd,
ABN 70 001 002 357).
Visit the Heinemann Library website @
www.heinemannlibrary.com.au

First published in Great Britain by Raintree,
Halley Court, Jordan Hill, Oxford OX2 8EJ,
part of Harcourt Education.
Raintree is a registered trademark of Harcourt Education Ltd.

R̄ A Reed Elsevier company

© Reed International Books Australia Pty Ltd 2004

08 07 06 05 04
10 9 8 7 6 5 4 3 2 1

Editorial: Carmel Heron, Sandra Balonyi
Design: Stella Vassiliou, Marta White
Photo research: Jes Sendbergs, Wendy Duncan
Production: Tracey Jarrett
Map: Guy Holt

Typeset in Officina Sans 19/23 pt
Pre-press by Digital Imaging Group (DIG)
Printed in China by WKT Company Limited

National Library of Australia Cataloguing-in-Publication data:
Pyers, Greg.
  Reef explorer.

  Bibliography.
  Includes index.
  For primary school students.
  ISBN 1 74070 145 3.

  1. Coral Reef ecology – Juvenile literature. I. Title.
  (Series : Pyers, Greg. Habitat explorer).

577.789

Acknowledgements
The publisher would like to thank the following for permission to reproduce photographs: ANT Photo Library/Norbert Wu: p. 11, /Kelvin Aitken: pp. 15, 27, /Natural Images: p. 24, /Cyril Webster: p. 25; Auscape/Ben Cropp: p. 19, /Ben & Lynn Cropp: p. 6, /Mark Spencer: p. 26, /David Wachenfeld: p. 14; courtesy of the Great Barrier Reef Marine Park Authority: pp. 13, 17, 18, 28, 29; Great Southern Stock/Mary Malloy: p. 10; Lochman Transparencies /John & Val Butler: p. 16; marinethemes.com/Kelvin Aitken: pp. 5, 8, 12, 20, 21, 22, 23; PhotoDisc: p. 9.

Cover photograph of turtle reproduced with permission of PhotoDisc; photograph of coral reef reproduced with permission of Marine Themes/Kelvin Aitkin.

Every attempt has been made to trace and acknowledge copyright. Where an attempt has been unsuccessful, the publisher would be pleased to hear from the copyright owner so any omission or error can be rectified.

Contents

Any words appearing in the main text in bold, **like this**, are explained in the Glossary.

Great Barrier Reef

Imagine sitting on a boat, floating over the Great Barrier Reef, off the north-eastern coast of Australia. The water is clear and calm. You check that your wetsuit is zipped up and that your oxygen tank is secure. You will need the tank to breathe underwater. You put on your goggles, bite on your breathing mouthpiece, and tumble backwards into the sea.

This map shows the locations of the world's coral reefs. Coral reefs are found in warm, shallow, tropical seas around the world.

4

Colour and movement

The bubbles clear and you have your first view of the reef. Everywhere there are fish, some swimming in schools, and others cruising alone. A green turtle is feeding on **algae** growing on a rock. A crab darts for cover.

All around you is coral. There are huge coral spikes that look like antlers, coral plates as big as tables, and lumps of coral that look like huge brains.

Coral reef habitats

Coral reefs provide many places for animals and plants to live. These places are called **habitats**.

Brightly coloured fish are a feature of coral reefs.

Making coral

You glide through a coral gully. The different corals are crowded together like shrubs in a garden display. But the coral is hard, like rock. This amazing structure is built by an animal, with help from a plant.

Even a small section of reef has several different types of coral.

Coral shapes:
- brains
- antlers
- fans
- flowers
- domes
- stacks.

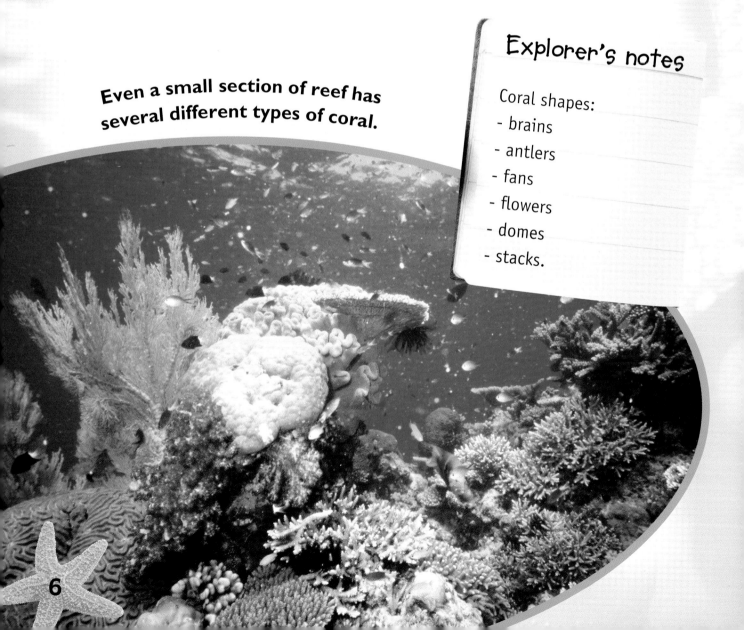

6

The coral polyp is the animal that builds the reef.

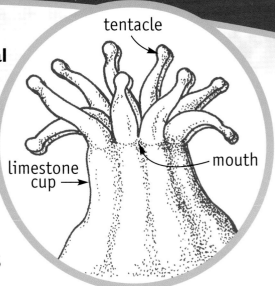

tentacle

mouth

limestone cup

Polyps

Coral is mainly limestone, built by tiny animals called polyps. Each polyp takes salts from the sea and changes them to limestone. The polyp uses this limestone to form a protective cup around its soft body. New polyps bud from each old polyp, then build limestone cups of their own. When the old polyp dies, it leaves behind its limestone cup. Over thousands of years, the layers build up and form a coral reef. Only the outer layer of coral has living coral polyps.

Algae and polyps

Living inside each coral polyp is a tiny **alga**, a simple plant. The polyp and the alga help each other. The alga produces sugars and oxygen, which the polyp uses to grow. The alga is protected inside the polyp and uses the polyp's wastes for its own growth. The alga needs sunlight to live. This is why coral grows in shallow, clear seas.

Biodiversity

The variety of life around you is amazing. One reason why so many **species** live in coral reefs is that there are many different kinds of **habitats** there. Another reason is that coral reefs are very old, which means that there has been a lot of time for many different kinds of animals to develop their own way of life among the coral.

Explorer's notes

Coral reef habitats:
- among the coral
- rocky crevices
- sandy sea floor
- open water
- **sea grass**
- coral islands.

More species of animals live in coral reefs than anywhere else in the sea.

Reptile diversity

Six marine turtle **species**, 17 seasnake species and the saltwater crocodile live in the waters of the Great Barrier Reef. They are all reptiles.

Biodiversity of reefs

Biodiversity is a word meaning the number of species in a particular area. Coral reefs have a very high level of biodiversity. In the Great Barrier Reef there are at least 1500 species of fish, 1500 sponges, 5000 molluscs (snails, prawns, slugs, octopuses) and 800 echinoderms (sea urchins, sea stars). There are also 400 species of coral polyps.

Green turtles feed on algae that grow in and around coral reefs.

9

Animal partnerships

A pair of clown fish catches your eye. While other fish dart away as you approach, these two keep close to what looks like a type of plant growing among the coral. You stop, and the fish retreat among its soft, swaying arms.

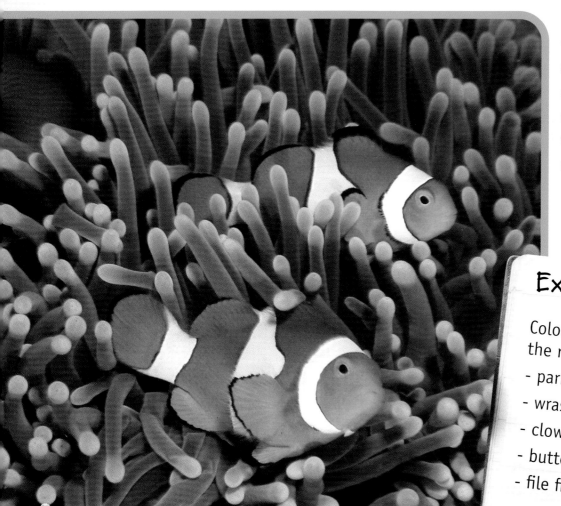

Clown fish are safe among the stinging tentacles of an anemone.

Explorer's notes

Colourful fish of the reef:
- parrot fish
- wrasse
- clown fish
- butterfly fish
- file fish.

The 'plant' is actually an **anemone**, which is like a large polyp. Its arms are stinging **tentacles** that stun tiny animals and then push them to its mouth. The stings also protect the anemone from fish that might want to eat it. But the clown fish are not affected by the stings, and so they keep close to the anemone for protection. This helps the anemone, which feeds on scraps dropped by the clown fish. Many animals and plants depend on each other for survival like this.

Cleaner wrasse

Cleaner wrasse are fish that feed on the **parasites** of larger fish. Parasites are animals that live on or in other animals. The large fish wait while the wrasse get to work removing these pests from gills, mouths and scales.

Hiding places

Among the coral are many nooks and crannies. As you approach, all sorts of animals dart away to hide in these places. One hundred or more damsel fish are feeding among the branches of an antler coral. You swim nearer and, in an instant, they dive out of sight. When you have passed, they come out again to feed.

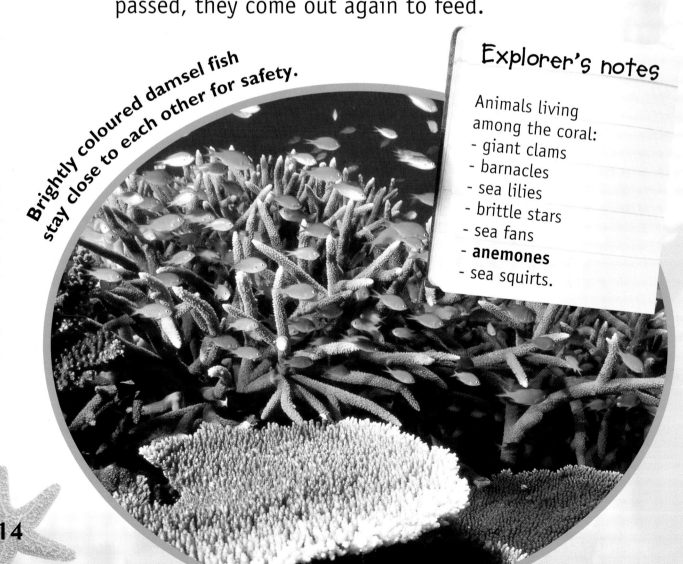

Brightly coloured damsel fish stay close to each other for safety.

Close encounter

There's a dark **crevice** in a rocky outcrop. This narrow gap in the coral is big enough to put your arm into, but you dare not. Who knows what might lurk in that mysterious place? A triggerfish passes between you and the crevice. Suddenly, a two-metre-long moray eel shoots out of the crevice as fast as a striking snake. The triggerfish struggles, but it is caught.

Whitetip reef sharks

Whitetip reef sharks spend the daylight hours sleeping in groups in coral caves. At night, they come out to hunt. Sharks are found in coral reefs around the world.

A moray eel grabs its prey in its sharp backward-curving teeth.

Giants of the reef

You squeeze through a gap in the coral and emerge into an area of open water. Suddenly, a shadow glides overhead. You look up and see a manta ray.

The manta ray is six metres across, but it is harmless. It flaps its huge fins and flies through the water with its mouth wide open. Sea water moves in through the ray's mouth and then out through its gills. The gills act like a sieve, catching tiny animals and plants, which are then swallowed.

Plankton

The tiny animals and plants that drift through the waters of the coral reef are called **plankton**.

The manta ray is one of the largest animals of the reef.

Danger!

Of all the large animals of the coral reef, the tiger shark is the most dangerous. It may grow to six metres and has rows of razor-sharp teeth. Tiger sharks will attack just about anything, from large fish to turtles to divers who get too close!

Explorer's notes

Sharks of the reef:
- wobbegongs
- tiger sharks
- angel sharks
- hammerhead sharks
- whitetip reef sharks.

The triangle-shaped teeth of a tiger shark are extremely sharp.

19

The sandy bottom

Below you is a stretch of sandy seabed. There seem to be very few animals moving down there. You see a crab wandering over the sand. Its pincers are busily picking up tiny scraps of dead plants and animals and putting them in its mouth. The crab takes another step and ... suddenly, the sand erupts! A large fish appears and, in a flash, the crab is gone.

Sea slugs

Sea slugs crawl over the sand to feed on dead animal or plant matter. If attacked, they can push out their internal organs into the sea to confuse a **predator**. Within weeks, the sea slug grows a new set of organs.

The wobbegong has a dense body, which enables this shark to lie in the sea floor.

Hidden predators

The fish was a wobbegong, a kind of shark. With its flat body and mottled skin, this **predator** is very well **camouflaged** against the sandy seabed of a coral reef.

This angel shark has just caught a fish called a yellowtail scad.

Angel sharks also lie flat on the sand, waiting to catch any passing crab, octopus or fish.

Explorer's notes

Animals of the sandy seabed:
- sea urchins
- worms
- sea snails
- crabs
- sponges
- stingrays.

Sea meadows

Covering a sandy seabed between two coral reefs is a large area of green plants. It looks like an underwater meadow. In the distance, a cloud of sand billows up into the clear water. You move closer to investigate.

Now you see it – a **dugong**, moving slowly over the sea floor. More sand billows as the dugong takes a mouthful of plants and rips them out to eat.

A dugong closes its nostrils tight when feeding underwater.

Manatee

The manatee lives in the Caribbean Sea, off the east coast of North America. This animal is very similar to the dugong. It feeds on plants of the sea floor, and sometimes enters rivers to feed.

Underwater flowering plants

These plants are **sea grass**. The calm waters of the coral reef are excellent **habitats** for this flowering plant. Rough seas would smother the plants or uproot them. Sea grass needs sunlight to grow so it is found in shallow water. Dugongs eat almost nothing but sea grass and so they are found all along the Great Barrier Reef.

Sea grasses provide hiding places for many small animals.

A coral cay

The water is just one metre deep now. It is low tide and you are about to step ashore on an island. This is a coral **cay** (pronounced 'key'), an island made of coral and sand laid down over thousands of years. The coral is nothing more than rock now, but the cay is alive with thousands of birds.

Coral cays of Belize

There are more than 1000 coral cays along the coral reefs of Belize, in Central America. Many of these cays are important nesting places for **endangered** marine turtles, such as the loggerhead turtle.

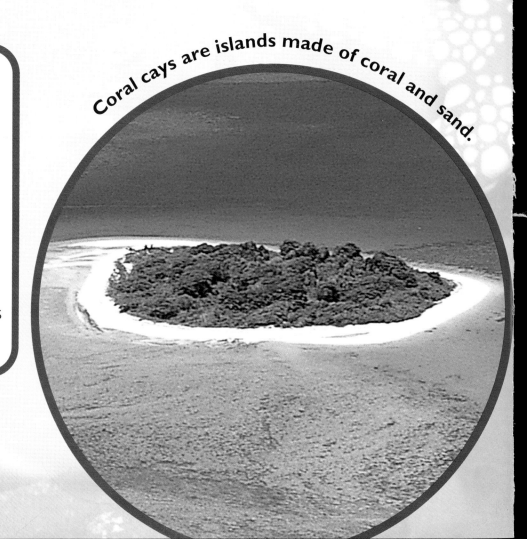

Coral cays are islands made of coral and sand.

Sea birds of the coral cays

Many sea birds use coral cays for nesting and resting. During the day, the birds feed at sea, but at night they return to the cays.

About 70 000 black noddies nest on one cay on the Great Barrier Reef.

Because coral cays have very little soil, few plants can grow there. In the breeding season, sooty terns lay their eggs in the sand. Black noddies pack seaweed together to make their nests.

Explorer's notes

Birds of coral cays:
- noddies
- terns
- frigatebirds
- tropicbirds
- boobies.

The reef at night

The sun sets quickly. An almost-full moon lights your way back into the water.

The first thing you notice about the reef at night is the coral itself. It seems to have lost its hard appearance. During the day, coral polyps stay hidden within their limestone cups. But at night, they stretch out their **tentacles** to catch **plankton** drifting by. With millions of tentacles waving, the coral surface is fuzzy and soft.

These mushroom leather corals have fully extended their stinging tentacles to catch prey.

Reproduction

The water is becoming cloudy. The coral is squirting millions of tiny balls and milky liquid into the water. This is a rare event that happens only at night, after a full moon. The coral is **reproducing**.

It is **eggs** and **sperm** that are being released into the sea. When one egg and one sperm meet, a **larva** is formed. One day, this tiny animal may settle in the right spot and begin making new coral.

When corals spawn, the sea becomes cloudy.

Future of coral reefs

Coral reefs do not live forever. Over millions of years, they have come and gone as the climate and sea levels changed. But today, many of the world's coral reefs are under threat from human activities. These activities include dynamiting to catch fish, and coral collecting by tourists. Even what people do on land is affecting coral reefs.

Anchor chains of boats can cause serious damage to coral.

Coral bleaching

From time to time, large areas of coral reef turn white, when the polyps spit out their algae. This is called **coral bleaching**. It happens when the polyps are under stress from a rise in sea temperature.

28

Silt

Land-clearing can cause large amounts of **silt** to flood into the sea. Silt can smother the coral and block out the sunlight. The coral **algae** die and so do the polyps. Sometimes, chemicals from farmland reach the reef. The chemicals cause so much seaweed to grow that the coral is smothered and dies.

Learning about coral reefs helps us understand and protect them.

Saving coral reefs

More than 80 countries are working together in the Global Coral Reef Monitoring Network to protect coral reefs from human activities that damage them.

Explorer's notes

Threats to coral:
- silt
- farm chemicals
- dynamiting
- souvenir-collecting
- damage by boats
- rising sea temperatures.

You may have the opportunity to visit a coral reef. If you do, observe the different kinds of habitats you see. Observe the animals and plants you see in these places. Note how many different kinds of coral there are.

Using the Internet

Explore the Internet to find out more about coral reefs. Websites can change, so if the link below no longer works, don't worry. Use a kid-friendly search engine, such as www.yahooligans.com or www.internet4kids.com, and type in keywords such as 'coral reef', or even better, the name of a particular coral reef or animal.

Website

www.gbrmpa.gov.au
The Great Barrier Reef Marine Park Authority website has information on all aspects of the Great Barrier Reef Marine Park and World Heritage Area.

Glossary

adaptation feature of an animal or plant that helps it to survive

alga (plural: algae) plant without roots or sap

anemone sea animal with stinging tentacles

biodiversity variety of living things in a certain area

camouflage colours and patterns that help an animal to hide in its habitat

cay island formed by coral

coral bleaching whitening of coral when sea temperatures increase

crevice narrow crack

dugong large marine mammal that feeds on sea grass

egg female cell

endangered in danger of becoming extinct

habitat place where an animal or a plant lives

larva (plural: larvae) young form of many animals

parasite animal or plant that lives on or in another animal and benefits from it

plankton tiny animals and plants that drift in the sea

predator animal that kills and eats other animals

reproduction producing and raising young

sac small bag-like part of an animal

sea grass flowering plant of shallow seas

silt fine particles of sand and rock

spawning releasing eggs and sperm

species group of living things that reproduce with each other

sperm (plural: sperm) male cell

tentacle long arm or feeler on an animal's body

venom poison

Index